Far Other

Poems

Cameron Morse

Also by Cameron Morse:

Baldy from Spartan Press

Terminal Destination from Spartan Press

Coming Home with Cancer from Blue Lyra Press

Father Me Again from Spartan Press

Fall Risk from Glass Lyre Press

Far Other

Poems by
Cameron Morse

Woodley Press

2020

Copyright ©2020 by Cameron Morse
All rights reserved, including right of reproduction in whole or part in any form.

Printed in the United States of America

Published by Woodley Press, Washburn University, Topeka, KS

Cover art: *Saint Francis Adoring a Crucifix*, Guido Reni, 1631-1632, The Nelson-Atkins Museum of Art, Kansas City, MO

Typesetting, layout, and cover design: Greg Field

ISBN 978-0-9987003-9-7

Library of Congress Cataloging-in-Publication data

woodleypress.org

For my daughter Naomi Mira, a.k.a. Omidon

Acknowledgments

I would like to thank Al Ortolani, my copyeditor Melissa Fite Johnson, and the rest of the Woodley Press editorial board for adopting the manuscript for this book. I am also grateful to the editors in whose magazines the following poems first appeared (some in earlier forms):

8 Poems: "Dongguan"
Blue Moon Literary & Art Review: "Corporeality"
Communion Arts Journal: "Anticonvulsant"
The Cresset: "On *Saint Francis Adoring a Crucifix* by Guido Reni"
Dappled Things: "Room," "Shadow Loves"
Edison Literary Review: "House Church"
Evocations: "Taking Leave of a Pesticide Applicator"
HeartWood Literary Magazine: "Magenta after Magenta"
I-70 Review: "To the Patron Saint of Phlebotomy"
The Indianapolis Review: "Description of a Typical Day
    for My Continuing Disability Report"
Leaping Clear: "A Kind of Presence"
Lotus-eater: "Self-Quarantine"
Mason Street: "Sameness"
MockingHeart Review: "Repose with Golden Retriever"
Modern Literature: "The Milk Thou Givest"
Naugatuck River Review: "Father Christmas"
New Feathers Anthology: "The Consistency of Snow"
NEW TEXAS: "Social Distancing"
North of Oxford: "Burr Oak Woods," "Crucifixion of a Phantasm"
The Opiate: "Stay-at-Home Order," "Back Yard Elegy"
Pirene's Fountain: "Seldom Is"
Rabid Oak: "Homestead"
Sou'wester: "We All Scream for Ice Cream"
STONECROP MAGAZINE: "Anastasia"
thimble: "Time Lapse"
thimble (newsletter): "Frequencies," "Home Loan Application"
TYPO: "Day of My First Seizure"
Viva Brevis: "Baby's First Spring"
Whale Road Review: "A Lowly Habitation"

Not this ordinary light, which all flesh may look upon, nor as it were a greater of the same kind, as though the brightness of this should be manifold brighter, and with its greatness take up space. Not such was this light but other, yea, far other from these.

Saint Augustine

Contents

Acknowledgments	vi
Repose with Golden Retriever	1

I

Room	5
Day of My First Seizure	7
To the Patron Saint of Phlebotomy	8
Description of a Typical Day for My Continuing Disability Report	9
Time Lapse	10
Anticonvulsant	11
On *Saint Francis Adoring a Crucifix* by Guido Reni	12
Father Christmas	13
Stay-at-Home Order	14

II

Dongguan	17
Anastasia	19
The Consistency of Snow	20
Taking Leave of a Pesticide Applicator	21
We All Scream for Ice Cream	22
Back Yard Elegy	23
Shadow Loves	24

The Milk Thou Givest	25
Seldom Is	26

III

Burr Oak Woods	29
Crucifixion of a Phantasm	30
A Kind of Presence	31
Corporeality	32
Hottest Sports Cars	33
Self-Quarantine	34
Social Distancing	35
For the Best	36

IV

A Lowly Habitation	39
Easter Sunday in the Emergency Room	40
Frequencies	42
House Church	43
Baby's First Spring	44
Home Loan Application	45
Sameness	47
Magenta after Magenta	48
Homestead	50
Notes	52

Far Other

Repose with Golden Retriever

Awaken me to delight,
I am so thoroughly

exhausted, so bored
of my poems, my manuscripts.

        4:53PM December sunset, twilight soon to ensue.

Third trimester, Lili counts down to
the New Year, a girl
baby in her outstretched belly.

        Raise, entice me, old dog with the whitening face.

Drop your tennis ball at my feet,
your ratty old rubber fuzz

with the split jacket, the scalped
forehead. Invite my hurt
hand, my tattered knuckle skin.

        Let me smooth your amber mane.

I

Room

> *What room is there in me,*
> *whither my God can come into me?*
> *—Saint Augustine*

The room is here. I am
making room in this

moment, my computer
closed, my two-year-old

asleep, all the people
noises behind me.

I am making room,
Augustine, I am scooting

over on the bench, I am
vacuuming the carpet.

What, though, when God is
the bench? What when

God is the carpet? The afghan
I spread over my legs?

Heaven and earth, you ask,
do they contain Thee? Out here,

where it is warm in December,
I am wearing a gray hood

over my head, brown slippers
over my feet. The striped

afghan draped over my legs
has a history. Purchased

at a giftshop on Pikes
Peak the foggy day after my first

seizure and what have I been
making since then but room

for you, my God? I know
my time is limited. My time is

my room. This moment
is all the room I have.

Day of My First Seizure

In the morning I listened as the country mountain preacher cast down arguments and every high thing, then went with friends into Cripple Creek and ate a burnt hamburger among the rundown casinos. I wanted to spot the ancestral donkeys of the first gold miners which the townsfolk still allow to roam. The shame of it is, I didn't, and at the Heritage Museum wearied of prospector stories. At an ice-cream shop, I treated everybody to a scoop but me. A hailstorm sprang upon the two-lane highway back to Florissant. Ice balls burst into stars upon the windshield. Halfway up the gravel drive, I climbed out into the rain wearing a sister's sunbonnet to meet an antlered mule deer that was curled up below the Ponderosa pines. It returned my gaze. Moss-splotched slabs of pink granite darkened around us. Saucers of sugar water dangled from the ranch house eaves and hummingbirds fenced about them. After dark, lightning forked over Pikes Peak. The bones of dead deer flared up below the deck rail where I stood, scanning the twilit rise for mountain lions.

To the Patron Saint of Phlebotomy

Separate my platelets,
my lymphocytes, my red

blood cells. While I eat time
capsules decaled like model

airplanes, you build thunderheads
of scar tissue in my arm crook.

Five days a week, I swallow.
Your nosecones plunge into the pit

of my stomach, releasing
payloads of prayer beads. Five days

a week, I toss back my shot
of tequila, a Hail Mary.

I take the rat poison the way
I take my coffee, the way I take

my leave, drip by drop,
like an oil spill in the driveway.

Description of a Typical Day for My Continuing Disability Report

On a typical day, I wake up with cancer.
I spoon coconut oil onto polymer.
My iceberg of healthy natural

fat pirouettes above a spreading puddle.
If my cancer cells require glucose,
I give them ketones. I beat

ketones into my eggs. On a typical day,
I drink six cups of coffee,
pouring them out of my thermos, little

by little, into stoneware.
I reserve the morning of a typical day
for psalms of blastoma, the songs

of my cells, an uncontrollable
division of angels on the head of a pin,
the tip of a needle. I fill Moleskine

after Moleskine with the concrete details
of a typical day,
its dishes hot out of the washing machine,

the smell of laundry in the nostril
of the exhaust fan,
a rusty spade left out in the rain.

Time Lapse

Little pockets of light
                    in a hairy mass
overhead. Any point
              I look at, the mass
is moving. It is moving
                    everywhere I look.
You cannot imagine
      how much sky there is

      above me. It's amazing
      I'm not afraid.
                    The roof is alive.
It has little pockets
      of light, spots,
              and strips of orange
along the horizon graze
the dark junipers.

Look up again and the one
      cloud's broken into lots, a herd,
                    a pod of gray, gray
gray whales, and the sky between

      is vaguely blue again,   pastel,

interstitial,   outlining the glacially

      slow loss   of my life.

Anticonvulsant

Little tablet,
sky-blue

sacrament, paint
chip off the ceiling

of a cathedral,
I call you Keppra,

my Protector:
Levetiracetam.

Twice daily
your splinter

of stained glass
passes through the palm

of my hand.
Twice daily I accept

your gospel of 250 ml.
Transubstantiate

your body into my
blood, your word

into my flesh.
I accept

your side effects:
somnolence,

decreased energy,
suicide, salvation.

On *Saint Francis Adoring a Crucifix* by Guido Reni

Last night, at Inklings'
Books and Coffee Shoppe,
when you asked if I am ever going
to stop writing cancer poems

and pursue other subjects, I thought
of Saint Francis tonsured
at the Nelson-Atkins,
his cadaverous hands folded

over his breast like wings, how the right
hand rests upon the left, as if
to perform CPR on his own stopped
heart, the breath sucked out

of his lungs, his eyes flung open
at the moment of arrest, the moment
arrested, and may you never know
what it's like to be transfixed,

to don a stitched cassock and waft
like a dove in the updraft, caught up
in the representation of a death
which is also your own.

Father Christmas

Snow fleshes out the ribcages
of unraked oak leaves, wood pile

whitening like the dog's winter coat.
Makes me wonder if it's snowing in Yantai,

snowing over the Bohai Sea, where you live
with your new family called Forget, called Spirits,

called Loneliness. I remember your shaky
hands that last Christmas I visited.

Shaking with anger or Parkinson's, you thought
only of Parkinson's, women,

a shot of heroin to use in case of another
heart attack. That last walk

we took along the frozen coast, you were zipped
like a lumberjack in coveralls

and earmuffs. Looking back, I know
my tumor nestled even then

inside me, glial white in gray
matter, when our heartfelt debates about God

and the family garbage, gave way
to the tick of snowflakes.

Stay-at-Home Order

I am a child, Ambrose.
Today I celebrate my birth
during a pandemic.
In my conical party hat
I unwrap birthday presents
though I did not ask,
no one asks to be born.
I did not choose to be marooned
in my childhood home
other men strip of wood rot
and reframe, repaint, after
their own image. After they
have finished, it will be
as if I were never born. But OK,
I'm sometimes OK with that.
How many worlds had I gained
before the glottal stop clipped
short the Word I was born with?
What path is this my feet are
bared to? What phonemes
do the birds sing? How can I stay
home if I don't know what
home is anymore, what art is,
what Thou art, and I have
lost the trailhead? My steps
scattered like bits of bread
are not the Bread. I watch you
read, your eyes glissade, in silence.
Come to visit you, I leave
without hello, without goodbye.

II

Dongguan

My sister Mariah's breakfast
coincides with lunch,

    how the worst summer

of my life I nocturned
    on bootleg DVD's and instant noodles,

    knocked off novels (*Catch-22,
The Razor's Edge, Catcher

in the Rye, Seymour*).
    I lit cigarettes I hadn't figured out

    how to inhale and bought
my first box of condoms,

    averting the supermarket
    checkout girl's gaze

in the factory town of Dongguan
    where my missionary parents'

    marriage ruptured in the first
argument I ever heard them have.

Mom screaming behind the bedroom
door fainted that summer

while hanging clothes out on the balcony
of our rented rowhouse.

    Mangos plopped in the lane
    of the gated compound

    for the mistresses
of Hong Kong businessmen

while I shampooed the thinning crown
of my head from a quack

Chairman Mao lookalike
    labeled bottle.

I ran through my twenties.

    In Dongguan,
I hung the red t-shirt I pranced in

over the second-story rail.
    Mariah remembers this,

more than anything, stiffening
with sweat. I still can't believe the movies

we watched then: *The Exorcist, 28 Days
Later, Zodiac*: She only 12,

    now 26 night owls her way
    through grad school.

I rise early with the kids
but see myself as I was then

    ankles rolling
over the mashed sidewalks

    of machine shops.
Along the scum skirt canal,

I caught a thousand dark stares
with my milk white thighs.

Anastasia

After house church and the potluck lunch, you would wash dishes,

submerging ruddy hands in the sink of gray streaks.

I made myself your dryer and in that way we both escaped

the company of others, the prattle and gossip
of grownups, your father who poked his head in at times to say

*that's what I like to see, children hard
at work,* or some such nonsense.

                                        Why does my memory of this persist?

It comes back while I'm scrubbing
my son's tray with the soft side
of the sponge or wiping detergent into white
swirls on the grained cypress
cutting board Lili says can't weather
the washing machine.

       I would have preferred to stand with you there

at the altar of the countertop   receiving plate
after plate, bowl after bowl, for the rest
of my life, plain white ceramic dripping all over the muddy floor.

The Consistency of Snow

Commingling foot soles with paw pads
of dogs printing in snow
on the back patio, I time myself,
my time with Augustine,
against the white sand in the hourglass
of the sky, synchronizing
the afternoon naps of newborn
and two-year-old. Quite a feat to keep
this soul afloat with a little breath.
Quite an accomplishment
to know that God is Spirit. Is nothing
like me in my animal body. My mother-in-law
Facetiming from her ghost
town in Guizhou, her coronavirus
quarantined apartment. China,
no longer bustling, bristles with fear.
Errant otherwise housebound randoms
caught in the deserted grocery store
shun and shop in silence,
their snouts muzzled by gauze.
Entering the second month
of her maternity leave, Lili fills
storage bags of breastmilk
for the freezer, readying for her return
to the Montessori Children's House.
Her pump wheezes for a while
after each extraction, clearing out
the tubular sinuses, the valved membranes
of the breast shields. Outside,
on my hands and knees, I realize
how wrong I was about the sand simile.
The snow falling on stone is not granular.
It is splinters. Tiny white splinters
prickling green splotches of moss,
the fragments of a shattered door
to some celestial courtyard.

Taking Leave of a Pesticide Applicator

No longer the wild one, the wildebeest,
I have returned to my childhood home. It's my turn
to position myself and yours to leave me

standing in the driveway.
If I hadn't left you all those years ago
to your own devices in Yantai, where would we be today?

What tabasco sauce might we, as cohorts, have
snorted, what Xanax trips taken,
hanging onto our shirttails? If I hadn't left you

to secrecy of rain-drenched lips, twins
you kissed on a crowded bus by accident, they presumed,
the way my parents first slickened each other's faces,

would you have grown more poems, my good
gardener friend, patting down words in the dark soil
of your mind? There are riches I robbed you of,

every departure a stab wound, every betrayal a traitor's
love entrenched. My memory is we kissed
on Xanax, leaned across the aisle and locked lips,
harbored a case of Natural Ice on a dry campus.

You were always falling in love
with someone else. Now I understand
why you tried to break into that church at night,

triggering the alarm, and found God
in those flashing lights, the sensitive tip of the baton.
I was already gone.

We All Scream for Ice Cream

Next county rain
clouds blur like a carousel
of dark horses
along the horizon, a cataract
subsuming treetops
in whiteness, a windshield
clouded by fog. Headlights on
in late morning. Theo raises
a fallen leaf to the tree it fell from.

Metallic air boxes my ears, tar
tinged with rancor
mornings my prediabetic brother
scarfs cornbread and chocolate
ice cream before work. I scream
on the inside, remember
myself at seventeen, my senior year
apartment mate eating cold soup
out of a can. On the mattress
he dragged into the living room,
Nick begged for extensions
before dropping out.

Wind loosens a patter of acorns.

Squatting with Theo on a storm drain
across from the stale
cigarette duplexes of 6th street,
I spot a monarch among the leaves
that have gathered like crumbs
in the corner of a mouth.

Back Yard Elegy

Below freezing, I trawl the back yard like an old man in a straw
        raincoat on river snow. My morning coffee glazes
over with ice. Last winter's long johns lost,
        I wear pajama bottoms below blue jeans the old dog
imprints with his happy-to-see-me paws.

After instigating an unrequited make out session,
        he wants to crawl up
into my lap. I sit in the shadow
        of the house, in all that it has repressed, and weep.

        If the shadow of the king is the tyrant,
the wind's touch is like getting a massage from a dead lady
        on my first visit to the massage parlor with two hundred yuan
burning like a California wildfire in my pocket.

I could hear the clatter of Mahjong tiles, the blue jay's cry
        presaging its long low flight across the lawn. Old dog giving chase,
when will you learn to let things go?

Shadow Loves

In my twenties I too grew wild, Augustine, prowling
bar street hutongs in the shadow of the lighthouse.

    Now I shelter in the garage with a two-year-old.

There is so much static in the air out there, so many ghosts
floating in the statuary of snow, above and below me,

    where I crossed the three districts in a late night taxi,

answered one shadow on the balcony while another
waited in the bedroom. Surely my shadows

    grew, smoking hash in the dark attic where I smashed

my head on a rafter and bit off the kiss goodnight.
Surely some gnashed. Some bled.

    Some believed, calling me back after I fled my father's city

and married. Where are they now, my shadow loves?
Let the blizzard of my early years eat the orchard

    while I carry in the basketballs.

The Milk Thou Givest

Theo demands more
wheels. I comply with a panoply,
a daisy chain of shabby
rings cast beyond the undercarriage
of whatever truck I'm drawing,
I'm turning into a train
stretching across the horizon.
Omi brims with breastmilk.
Barf splotches adorn, they badge
the shoulder of every fleece or hoodie
I own. *What am I at best,*
you ask, *but an infant sucking
the milk Thou givest?* How malnourished am I
to my marrow? I no longer go
to the movies, thank God, one of parenting's
truly positive gains: An excuse to skip
any party. Pare away everything
but today's balming fragrant winter rain.
Shed the dream fragments
of snow, any sign of the colossal food
fight in which we wedding caked
ourselves. *Impermanence of desire,* indeed.
What blows my mind is why
the outside dog still tries to weasel
his muddy paws through the storm door
and spill into the house
that all my life I've wanted out of.

Seldom Is

Light slides along threads of spider web
loosened from last night's hooded
sweatshirt. That's God fingering the strings,
I guess, being pious for once.

Lili leaves me alone Sunday morning
to sulk in the empty driveway
and scan the lines of a lifetime of reading
for some kind of predictive rhythm.

She leaves with the boy, who wouldn't have it
any other way. Alone is seldom
for the stay-at-home dad, seldom is
the time I have to bang my head

against the idea of my never really being alone
because thy rod and thy staff they
comfort me and just like that, yes, I feel comforted.
The words unfurl from deep childhood

programming, a code I could never live by.
Patterns of shadow and light stitch their patchwork.
Give me a signal, Dad, patch me through
on a secure channel. I don't know how much longer

I can continue to listen to the white noise
of the stars, the squeal of a tile saw
across Duncan Road, or that one dog woofing in a hollow
place, that lone wolf in a place of echoes.

III

Burr Oak Woods

A walker in black leggings,
pink-dyed hair, raises her makeshift
mask to ask who stole her car,
where in the woods is
the parking lot that holds it.

Worn with cares and fears,
writes Augustine. A screenshot
from Facebook confirms
seven Costco workers COVID-19
where we buy pullups and wipes.

Bethany Falls Trail with Theo
for the first time, my son
emptying the spray bottle in his
mouth. My body unclenches
on a bench beside the gravel path.

All is stillness in the woods,
the oceanic wind surge, rat-a-tat
blast of somewhere a woodpecker,
faraway rumble of an airplane
lifting its crucifix over us

or against. For each passerby,
I yank my boy into the understory.
For great intervals of time,
there is only us. A single trunk
somewhere is creaking.

Crucifixion of a Phantasm

Spring rain self-quarantine
while you flay below *the scourge
of bodily sickness.* COVID-19
the topic of every breakfast, herd
immunity and high-dose Vitamin C,
how you refused baptism
even as your fever heightened,
Christ being nothing to you then
but *a phantasm.* Outside,
hyacinths purple dank mulch
with their royal robes.
Robins drop to the rippling bird bath
in the light-spangled orchard,
cardboard boxes sogging curbside
in recycling bins. I seize
upon the quarantine to learn the rules
for recycling, the new labels,
and rip the plastic window
screen from a box of spaghetti
noodles. Inhale the cleansing
chill of social distancing: school
closed, reading cancelled,
and today's sky doubtless is a kind
of phantasm, perhaps even
a phantasm crucified, for all I know.
Its pallor overwhelms me.

A Kind of Presence

A breeze rises in the night.
Moonflower leaves rattle in the arbor
behind my whitewashed
wicker chair, alerting me to a kind
of presence. My mother,

I imagine, back from work, hikes the dark
slope of the yard. A breeze
rises. Then there are only engines
moaning in their casements, their sheet
metal carapaces, and no breeze,

just the silence of the shriveled leaves
and whatever the stars have bequeathed me
of their light among the porch lit limbs
of the white oak rearing above. Some knowledge
would be the death of me. Some mornings

I can't squeeze my eyes
into the crow's feet of a smile, a greeting
for the hours to come. Why have I always had to know
everything? Now another breeze,
a colder kiss on the cheek, and the night

cars whisk, taillights streaking
bloodshot insomniacs peering between the dark pickets
of the fence that protects my privacy.

Corporeality

The sky drapes a staticky blanket
of needlepoints over my corporeal body.
Pricks that hail a rush of blood
into the sleep-fallen arm.

Day before the stay-at-home order goes into effect,
I lace my ears, conceal my mouth
with gauze. Each exhalation steams me blind
in my copper frames. A postal worker
shouts at me for invading the six feet required
for the next in line.

I conceived of things corporeal only,
confesses Augustine. Droplets of rain tingle
my uplifted face, the backs of my hands,
the cough that conducts the virus to the airways.

I conceive of raindrops as mist, the virus
as a white noise machine, the dark beehive Mom
planted in the hollow of the hallway

to drown out her marriage counseling
sessions, conducted in the bedroom. After Dad left,
she specialized in sexual addiction.

Hottest Sports Cars

Only my boy and I stir here, following the brick-and-mortar contours of the gymnasium into recesses of tinted glass, black screens that display us to ourselves: my shaggy temples, the exploded bird's nest of Theo's nap. I try a door handle. Demonstrate the lockdown. He forages a lost golf ball. Desperation hits when a Montessori classmate's mother tests positive and what choice for Lili but to work for the living we have and hope for the best? Better to be a lost golf ball than the lanyard clinking this flagless pole. Better to be downhill from the Walker Family Cemetery—hilltop copse for the dead shelterers of outlaw Jesse James—than interred in it and with my boy than alone, roaming Blue Springs the last summer of my solitude. Sitting side by side, we unfurl our first library book since the start of the pandemic—delivered through the car window by a masked librarian—and enter the pantheon of Ferrari, Lamborghini, Porsche.

Self-Quarantine

The streetlight is conspicuous
because of how bright it is.
Late March twilight. Still no mosquitoes
but some faint movement swarms
the orchard branches, grainy
leaps across a smoky sky. Already the resolution
not to go out has resulted in near
total chaos, decapitated lamps, sex dreams
and shouting matches at the butcher
block. I carry the recycling bins
out of the garage only to collide with my first
moment alone all day long. Tonight's air
is calm. Its current bursts
like static in my eye socket. Strips of cloud, salmon
pink, proclaim their grievances
to the horizon, darkening gables and the embery
glow of a kitchen window, the voices
of children shrilling in the cul-de-sac, a gang
of girls playing tag, screaming *tag
you're it*, as the shadows debut: the shadow
of my hand, my hooded head.

Social Distancing

Perhaps I, too, cannot be healed
except by believing. March afternoon

bright and cold as a coma, ember
of yesteryear a hole burnt in the seat

of the patio chair. Hay stalks spill
into the grass, shoots of green onion

wagging like antennae over the terracotta
rim of the flowerpot. Sun fevers

my forehead, another symptom,
ensconced in my army green hood

from Beijing. My tube socks beartrap
deep red grooves above my ankles.

My aging gums recede. *I kept my heart,*
confesses Augustine, *from assenting*

to any thing. When I find a hole
in my heel, I tear it open.

Fall headlong into the slaughter
of April, the second month

of social distancing. Wind rises,
raises a hand hard against my denimed

calves, stitched seam of yellow thread.
Worn out, I throw myself away.

For the Best

How many times had you asked me
if I was ready to throw away
my radiation mask before tying together
the handles of a white
plastic bag from Walmart and tossing it
this morning before work?

How many times before you stuffed
my headspace with wet diapers,
dried-out wipes, the torn open wrappers
of your nursing pads?

But off you go and here I stay, as always,
to scrabble and dig through the detritus
of fatherhood, the aftermath of radiation,
until I can see pea gravel in the crescent
crack in the bottom of the garbage can.

It doesn't matter how ready I am
to hear the gutter water tap within
the corrugated elbow of the downspout
and raise some kind of lament for
what I admit I'm not ready to let go of,

what I imagined being a trophy
encased in the glass box of the time
left to me, a cherished reminder
of my impending death and luck,
what terrific luck in this streak
of spring days unimpeded by rain

because you are my better judgment.
You who have always excelled at forgetting
are wounded the worse for my silly
remembrances, my nasty little poems.

IV

A Lowly Habitation

I expose my lowly
clay pot, my coat
of skin to the jolts
of the wind. Nubby
leaves of Chinese
parsley waggle
in the patio table pot.
I tend to my little plot
of flesh, peeling off
the polyester dress socks,
pulling on the crinkly
sleeves of a windbreaker.
Lowly as it is, I love my body
as Christ loved his
hands, his dark arboreal
recesses. It's a shock
to be born. Omi spends
most of her time screaming
at her body, its rolls of leg
fat, the creases in her groin.
I look down at the baby
in my arm crook, her kinked
brow, her mewling lower
lip. Theodore runs full
force into the driveway's
pained face, its painful way
of saying if you ask me
to hold you, I will texture
the palms of your hands,
splotch and bleed them,
not gladly or with any sort
of malice, but just because I am
a driveway and you are made
of screeching eels. Maybe
this touch of your knee
to my beautiful blend of tiny
stones is the essence, the gravel bed
of Christ below the wood
form of the cross.

Easter Sunday in the Emergency Room

Let this pill bug rumble
over my bare foot.

Fasten to my Christ flesh
a thousand tiny teeth.

A nursing home
of yellow toenails dwells

within these walls
of skin, these varicose

veins, a married estate,
a research study

on premature, antique
ejaculations.

Show me Jesus naked.
The first time I saw semen

I stumbled in midnight
Horn Creek family camp

confusion to the toilet.
My father held up the stain

to his face the way
he used to read our bedtime

stories. His glasses left
on the nightstand. Please

God tell me you enjoyed
your body, however

briefly. In the emergency room,
I watch a documentary

on crucifixion, olivewood
infused with heelbone,

while mud dries
its poultice to my blue

jeans, clay from the culvert
where I planted my elbow

and broke into a trinity
of butterflies: hysterical

laughter, nauseating pain
and good grief, the surprise.

Frequencies

During her first week, Naomi
will sometimes fall
into a sort of glassy-eyed
reverie, an intense
expression of listening
to a frequency
beyond my range, the wind
whistling in the pipe
holes of the basketball goal,
the snow crackling
below the interrogation light
of the sun. Little tridents
of a bird's footprints
on the front stoop. Burrs
of frost on the gate latch,
the wisteria vine. Whatever
it is she's picking up on,
whatever the secret whispered
in her ear, the room's so
quiet it could just explode.

House Church

A pill bug rolls along the garage door sill, antennae glimpsing leaf bits and catkins. In the family room, the virtual church service commences. A morning much like this, three weeks ago, I stepped in mud and split my olecranon process into three pieces. In the lawn chair, I let down my arm. Listen to its murmur of ache, its yips of pain. Out in the driveway, rain bruises the fractured blocks. A next-door neighbor resorts to mud-jacking. Others grind their tree stumps, their teeth. Now my elbow won't straighten. My answering machine messages go unanswered for days because of COVID. Another vision says your job search is futile. The bees in your inbox are buzzing but their hive queen made off with the congregation. Look no farther than the crab apple leaves rocking on their stems. Their flutter is something flighty. Something eyelid. X-ray is a crosshatch of seven screws, ethereal blue china plate of angry bone.

Baby's First Spring

Born in winter my new
born daughter has never seen
the spring. Squinting

at the cold window pane,
she has yet to feel the yellow dog
of the sun climb into her lap.

Winter winds clamp down
on her white wicker bassinet, they
enter her blood like floes

in the bird bath. Never before
today has the whole earth
aired out the folds in her neck.

Today's spring breezes dogear
the corner of the page
I'm writing to my daughter

about the spring while ancient
leaves tumble in the air
around me, whispering secrets

and promises I've never heard
spoken in my thirty
odd years, the tinkle of chimes,

charisma of heat, warm breath
nibbling an earlobe,
hyacinths spiraling away

their runaway green wheels
of tongues in the burnt-out flowerbed
I once believed was real.

Home Loan Application

Debt collectors and credit
lenders, triage scissors

glide flat-jawed
through the exam room

parting cotton pad
and co-bind. For two weeks,

the plaster cupping my elbow
pooled blood into a mud pit,

a pothole collecting brown
rainwater. For five years,

my wife and I have sheltered
in place, radiology-brittled,

riddled with children
we don't know what to do with.

Now the cast comes off, bares
my creases of red skin

imprinted labyrinthine
as the river system

of a fingertip. My prints
suggest a squiggly roadmap

to recovery
but there's no way out

of this beartrap. I get lost
looking for the scheduler's desk

in a forest of phone calls.
No physical therapist alive

will take my health insurance,
my firm assurance of yes,

I swear to God I'll pay you back.
Stretch the bruised banana

of my arm until it breaks. Even S.S.I.
is a needs based program.

Sameness

The same, always
the same are you here
waiting for me.

The drama of my life
a storm-tossed sailor
is right, Augustine.

Sameness, subside.
Let me subsist on this
moment   minted
in shadow   in sheaths

of grass   gone to seed
gone to God   with their grievances
to the burnt-out   socket

of the sun.   Envelope
in darkness   my furry little
rabbit's foot,   my trembling

morsel   of human flesh.

Let the shush   reverb
in my ribs   of cartilage.

Magenta after Magenta

because the dye was discovered the year of the battle

Stop trying
to make it work.

Don't try.

It will be all right.

Just melt. Allow your
self to melt.

Be moment,
water. Wait for

whatever: Whatever
knows best.

Bless. Be less.
Be little. Forget.

Death will be like this
forgetting, this

orange blank
behind your eyelids,

serviceberry pink,
almost magenta.

The sapling planted
for my unborn

daughter has berried

in an orchard
in Magenta, the color

of the Battle of I
close my eyes.

Bury me here.

Homestead

Something like the smell
of sunscreen suggests the swimming
pool of my boyhood
on another pesticidal morning
toward the end of June.

July is closing in, the month of the move,
the scheduled closing, the fees as yet
unknown. What will it cost
to own a house, what gain this ownership?

Again Augustine rolling and turning
on his chain chooses the conventicle
over the affianced bride and I wish
things were so clear-cut for me:

Catastrophe one way, tautology the other.

An inchworm swings by the thread
of its would-be cocoon. Light grabs the green
shoulders of its photosynthesizing
children. Since birth I have chosen.

I have planted my stake, my seed.
I have seeded and steaded and selved
myself here, belonging only
to this infestation of ants.

This dead smell about the garbage can
doubtless is the fledgling
that fell in before it could fly out
and called for God knows how long for rescue.

Notes

A good many of these poems riff off, echo, or otherwise interact with Edward Bouverie's 2012 Simon & Brown translation of *Confessions* by Saint Augustine:

Epigraph: *Not this ordinary light, which all flesh may look upon, nor as it were a greater of the same kind, as though the brightness of this should be manifold brighter, and with its greatness take up space. Not such was this light but other, yea, far other from these.* (111-112)

"Repose with Golden Retriever": *... and our heart is restless, until it repose in Thee.* (4)

"Room": *... and what room is there within me, whither my God can come into me?* (4)

"Stay-at-Home Order": *... what sweet joys Thy Bread had for the hidden mouth of [Ambrose's] spirit ... I neither could conjecture, nor had experienced ... Ofttimes when we had come (for no man was forbidden to enter ...) we saw him thus [in silence] reading to himself, and never otherwise; and having long sat silent (for who durst intrude on one so intent?) we were fain to depart.* (82)

"The Consistency of Snow": *And I knew not God to be a Spirit, not one who hath parts extended in length and breadth, or whose being was bulk; for every bulk is less in part than in the whole: and if it be infinite, it must be less in such part as is defined by a certain space, than in its infinitude; and so is not wholly every where, as Spirit, as God.* (39)

"Shadow Loves": *... and I dared to grow wild again, with these various and shadowy loves: my beauty consumed away, and I stank in Thine eyes; pleasing myself, and desirous to please in the eyes of men.* (22)

"The Milk Thou Givest": *... and what am I even at best, but an infant sucking the milk Thou givest?* (46)

"Burr Oak Woods": *I should choose to be myself, though worn with cares and fears; but out of wrong judgment; for, was it the truth?* (87)

"Crucifixion of a Phantasm": *For Thou hadst not forgiven me any of these things in Christ, nor had He abolished by His Cross the enmity which by my sins I had incurred with Thee. For how should He, by the crucifixion of a phantasm, which I believed Him to be?* (73)

"Corporeality": *But I, conceiving of things corporeal only, was mainly held down, vehemently oppressed and in a manner suffocated by those "masses"; panting under which after the breath of Thy truth, I could not breathe it pure and untainted.* (76)

"Social Distancing": *For I kept my heart from assenting to any thing, fearing to fall headlong; but hanging in suspense I was the worse killed.* (84)

"Easter Sunday in the Emergency Room": *So were we then ... exhorting [Nebridius] to become faithful, according to his measure, namely, of a married estate.* (144)

"A Lowly Habitation": *Thy Word ... in this lower world built for Itself a lowly habitation of our clay ... our coats of skin.* (116)

"Sameness": *For Thou art ever the same; for all things which abide not the same nor for ever, Thou for ever knowest in the same way.* (125)

"Homestead": *Thus soul-sick was I, and tormented, accusing myself much more severely than my wont, rolling and turning on my chain till that were wholly broken ....* (137)

Cameron Morse

Cameron Morse is the author of six collections of poetry. He lives in Independence, Missouri with his wife Lili and two children. His poems have been published in numerous magazines, including *New Letters, Bridge Eight, Portland Review* and *South Dakota Review*. His first collection, *Fall Risk*, won Glass Lyre Press's 2018 Best Book Award. He holds an MFA from the University of Missouri, Kansas City—and serves as Senior Reviews editor at *Harbor Review* and Poetry editor at Harbor Editions.

www.ingramcontent.com/pod-product-compliance
Lightning Source LLC
Chambersburg PA
CBHW031214090426
42736CB00009B/919